CLUCK

A book of happiness for chicken lovers

EXISLE
PUBLISHING

Introduction

More and more people are discovering that chickens bring more to our lives than just eggs. Watching chickens go about their daily business in the backyard is relaxing, and their group dynamics and bizarre behaviours are far more interesting to watch than anything on television.

Anyone with chickens will know that they're as prone to hijinks as any other pet. Whether it's laying eggs in beds, sneaking up on cats or scratching up a dust storm in the sunshine, chickens everywhere cause their owners delight, distress and bemusement in equal measure.

These endearingly strange creatures have unique personalities. Hens will often strut confidently into houses if the door is left open and make themselves right at home. They'll eat the cat's food right out of its bowl or hop up onto the couch for an afternoon snooze.

They're choosy about where they'll nest or roost too. It's not uncommon for one nest box to

become the 'favourite', with all others ignored, despite looking identical. A rooster may jam his body into one particular hole in the fence for no obvious reasons of comfort or convenience.

This book is a celebration of these quirky characters, with a mix of hilarious and serious quotes from people who have come to know that chickens are not the dim-witted, dull creatures that they're often made out to be. With quotes from figures such as Oscar Wilde, Mark Twain and Patti LuPone combined with proverbs from all around the world, *Cluck* is designed to bring you as much joy and happiness as chickens do.

Corn can't expect justice from
a court composed of chickens.

AFRICAN PROVERB

The key to everything is patience.
You get the chicken by hatching
the egg, not by smashing it.

ARNOLD H. GLASOW

If curiosity killed the cat,
I doubt it spared the chicken.

ANONYMOUS

What of the hens whom we observe each day at home, with what care and assiduity they govern and guard their chicks? Some let down their wings for the chicks to come under; others arch their backs for them to climb upon; there is no part of their bodies with which they do not wish to cherish their chicks if they can, nor do they do this without a joy and alacrity which they seem to exhibit by the sound of their voices.

PLUTARCH

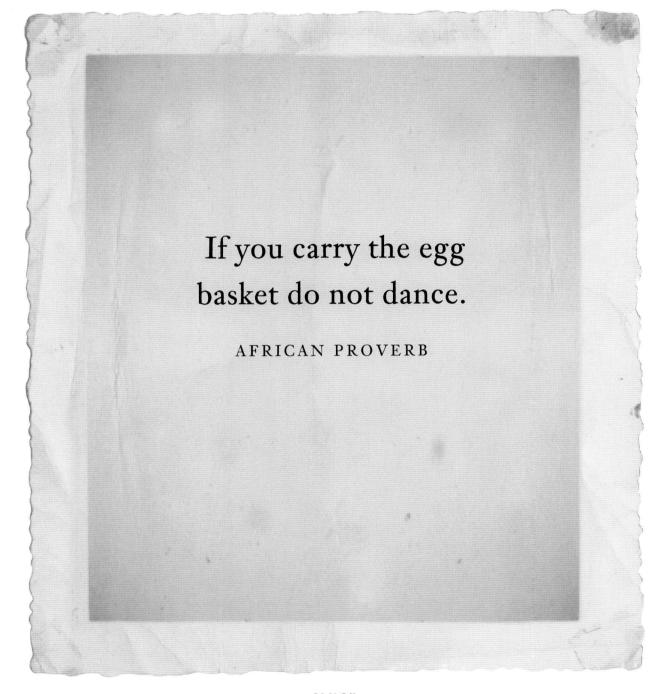

If you carry the egg
basket do not dance.

AFRICAN PROVERB

It may be hard for an egg to turn into a bird: it would be a jolly sight harder for it to learn to fly while remaining an egg. We are like eggs at present. And you cannot go on indefinitely being just an ordinary, decent egg. We must be hatched or go bad.

C.S. LEWIS

A true friend is someone who thinks that you are a good egg even though he knows that you are slightly cracked.

BERNARD MELTZER

If you were born lucky, even
your rooster will lay eggs.

RUSSIAN PROVERB

An egg today is better than
a hen tomorrow.

BENJAMIN FRANKLIN

People who count their chickens before they are hatched, act very wisely, because chickens run about so absurdly that it is impossible to count them accurately.

OSCAR WILDE

A chicken with beautiful plumage does not sit in a corner.

AFRICAN PROVERB

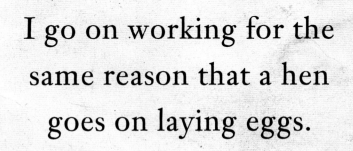

I go on working for the
same reason that a hen
goes on laying eggs.

H.L. MENCKEN

You can't expect a big egg
from a little hen.

IRISH PROVERB

We can see a thousand miracles around us every day. What is more supernatural than an egg yolk turning into a chicken?

S. PARKES CADMAN

Even clever hens sometimes
lay their eggs among nettles.

DANISH PROVERB

I'm convinced that some of those chickens that I preached to during the forties and the fifties tended to listen to me much better than some of my colleagues listen to me today in Congress. And some of those chickens were just a little more productive. At least they produced eggs.

JOHN LEWIS

He thinks the sun comes up
just to hear him crow.

SOUTHERN SAYING

In my experience, previously counted chickens never do hatch.

MARK TWAIN

THE CODFISH

The codfish lays ten thousand eggs,
The homely hen lays one.
The codfish never cackles
To tell you what she's done.
And so we scorn the codfish,
While the humble hen we prize,
Which only goes to show you
That it pays to advertise.

ANONYMOUS

Chickens are like nature's tea cozies. Eggs, pile of rocks, kittens, doesn't matter. You put it under them and by Jove, they will keep it warm.

REUBEN W.

My chicken is good, but my neighbour's looks better.

ROMANIAN PROVERB

I was just so drawn to the chickens in a way I can't articulate … Watching them take a dust bath was the most appealing and enchanting thing. Everything about them is so moving to me.

KAREN DAVIS

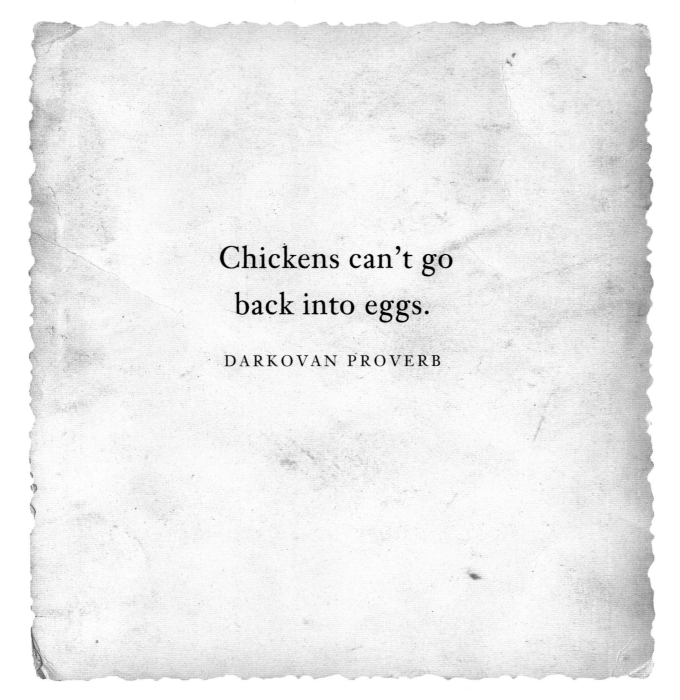

Chickens can't go
back into eggs.

DARKOVAN PROVERB

The sun has a right to 'set'
where it wants to, and so,
I may add, has a hen.

ARTEMUS (CHARLES FARRAR
BROWNE) WARD

Big chickens don't peck
at small seeds.

CHINESE PROVERB

Chickens have an uncanny
sense of direction.

DANIEL PINKWATER, *LIZARD MUSIC*

Unlaid eggs are uncertain chickens.

GERMAN PROVERB

Do not take life too seriously.
You will never get out of it alive.

ELBERT HUBBARD

A hen is heavy
when carried far.

IRISH PROVERB

Pride's chickens have bonny feathers, but they are an expensive brood to rear. They eat up everything, and are always lean when brought to market.

ALEXANDER SMITH

The hen knows that dawn has arrived but it leaves the duty of crowing to the cock.

AFRICAN PROVERB

You'll find that humans 'chicken out' more often than chickens do.

ANONYMOUS

Man is harder than a stone and
more brittle than an egg.

BULGARIAN PROVERB

Any chicken keeper can tell you that raising chickens is like eating potato chips: one is just not enough.

MEREDITH SKYER

The chicken that crows the loudest does not always give the biggest eggs.

FRENCH PROVERB

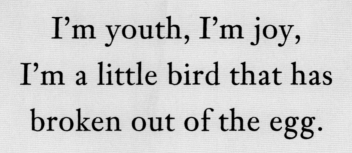

I'm youth, I'm joy,
I'm a little bird that has
broken out of the egg.

J.M. BARRIE, *PETER PAN*

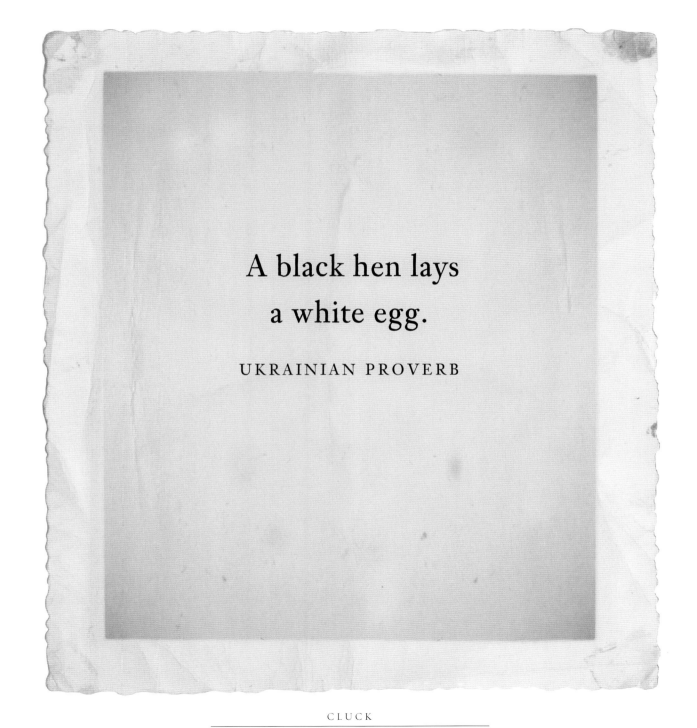

A black hen lays a white egg.

UKRAINIAN PROVERB

Get hens, get happy.

ANONYMOUS

A chicken that hatches
a crocodile's eggs is looking
for trouble.

MALAGASY PROVERB

It is not only fine feathers
that make fine birds.

AESOP

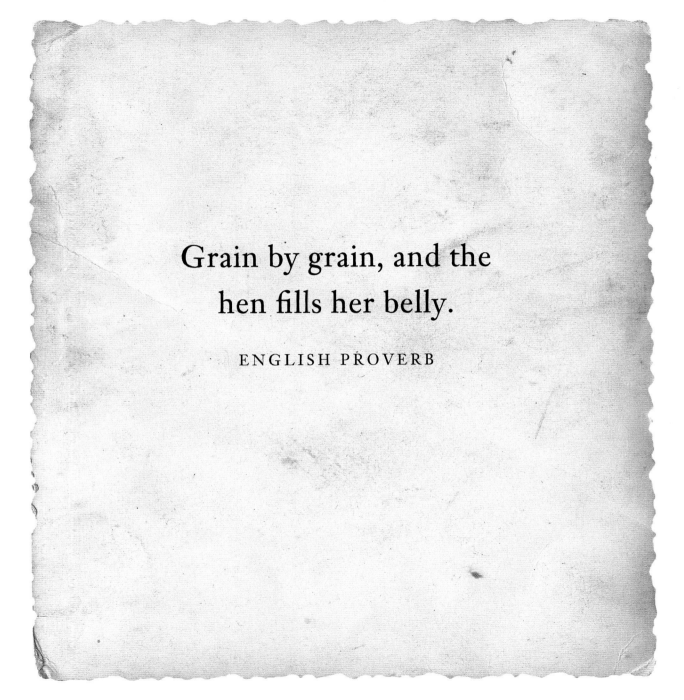

Grain by grain, and the
hen fills her belly.

ENGLISH PROVERB

It has, I believe, been often remarked, that a hen is only an egg's way of making another egg.

SAMUEL BUTLER

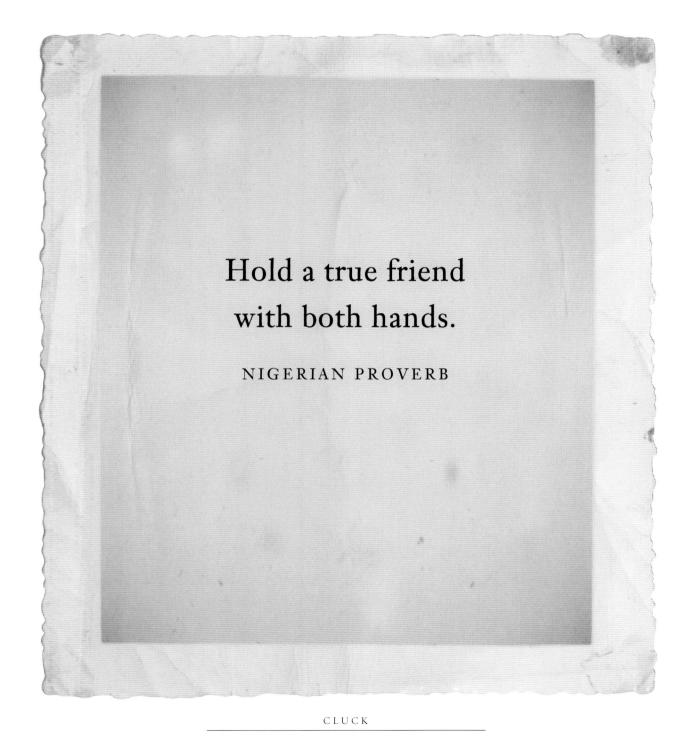

Hold a true friend
with both hands.

NIGERIAN PROVERB

CLUCK

Chickens are the gateway animal ...
It all starts off so innocently. You just
want to try having a few chickens ...
and next thing you know, you've got
turkeys, ducks, rabbits, goats, pigs,
cows, llamas and a pony.

LORI HERNANDEZ, THREE ACRE FARM

Prepare a nest for the hen and she will lay eggs for you.

PORTUGUESE PROVERB

The cocks may crow,
but it's the hen that
lays the egg.

MARGARET THATCHER

If an egg is broken by outside force, life ends. If broken by inside force, life begins. Great things always begin from inside.

JIM KWIK

When chickens luxuriate in sunlight, you'll rush out to make sure your chicken friend is still alive. They think it is hilarious when you do this. You don't.

MARJI BEACH

Use what talents you possess;
The woods would be very
silent if no birds sang there
except those that sang best.

HENRY VAN DYKE

A bird does not change its feathers
because the weather is bad.

NIGERIAN PROVERB

First ponder, then dare.

HELMUTH VON MOLTKE

Trust me, chicken keepers
LOVE to talk about
their chickens

LARA COLLEY, A MOUNTAIN HEARTH

Look not in last year's nests
for this year's birds.

MIGUEL DE CERVANTES SAAVEDRA,
WIT AND WISDOM OF DON QUIXOTE

It sometimes looks as if the chief products of my garden were small boys and hens.

CHARLES DUDLEY WARNER

The cock with lively din
Scatters the rear of darkness thin

JOHN MILTON, *L'ALLEGRO*

A person often meets his destiny on
the road he took to avoid it.

JEAN DE LA FONTAINE

To love deeply in one direction makes us more loving in all others.

ANNE SOPHIE SWETCHINE

Keeping animals, I have
learned, is all about water.
Who even knew chickens
drank water? I didn't, but
they do, and a lot.

SUSAN ORLEAN

When it's bed time I call them and they come running like any other pet, no matter where they are!

NANCY BIRTWHISTLE

I just love chickens.

PATTI LUPONE

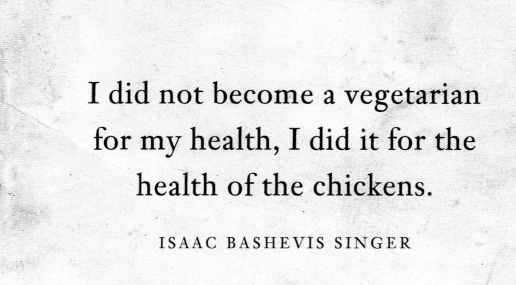

I did not become a vegetarian for my health, I did it for the health of the chickens.

ISAAC BASHEVIS SINGER

I try to keep them out of the veg-growing areas for much of the year, though ... on occasion they get in anyway and excavate the carrot beds or the newly planted raspberry canes ... but our garden is a family garden and they are family!

PIPPA GREENWOOD

The three sharpest things on earth: a hen's eye after grain, a blacksmith's eye after a nail and an old woman's eye after her son's wife.

IRISH PROVERB

I had almost three acres of land in Beverly Hills. And I had a big atrium of chickens because I love that feeling of being in the country and living from the soil.

EARTHA KITT

My parents made no money whatsoever, but they really knew how to see, as artists. So a big adventure might be, on a hot, dreadful day with no place to go, to go out and draw our chickens with pastels. My parents gave me a sense of wonder.

ALI MACGRAW

I haven't checked, but I highly suspect that chickens evolved from an egg-laying ancestor, which would mean that there were, in fact, eggs before there were chickens. Genius.

TA-NEHISI COATES

He is a wise man who does
not grieve for the things
which he has not, but rejoices
for those which he has.

EPICTETUS

I remember, as a kid, I'd follow the rooster and the chickens and watch what type of grass they'd eat. And me and my friends would eat that grass, like that was our lunch.

ADAM BEACH

If I hadn't started painting,
I would have raised chickens.

GRANDMA MOSES

The journey of a thousand miles
begins with a single step.

LAO TZU

I dream of a better tomorrow,
where chickens can cross the road
and not be questioned about
their motives.

RALPH WALDO EMERSON

While cats can be
infuriating, little old women
in fur coats, they make me
laugh. Of course, dogs,
horses and my highly social
chickens are dear to me, too.

RITA MAE BROWN

I love the feeling of the fresh air
on my face and the wind blowing
through my hair.

EVEL KNIEVEL

I also love to fantasize about
keeping chickens in the backyard.

KATHERINE CENTER

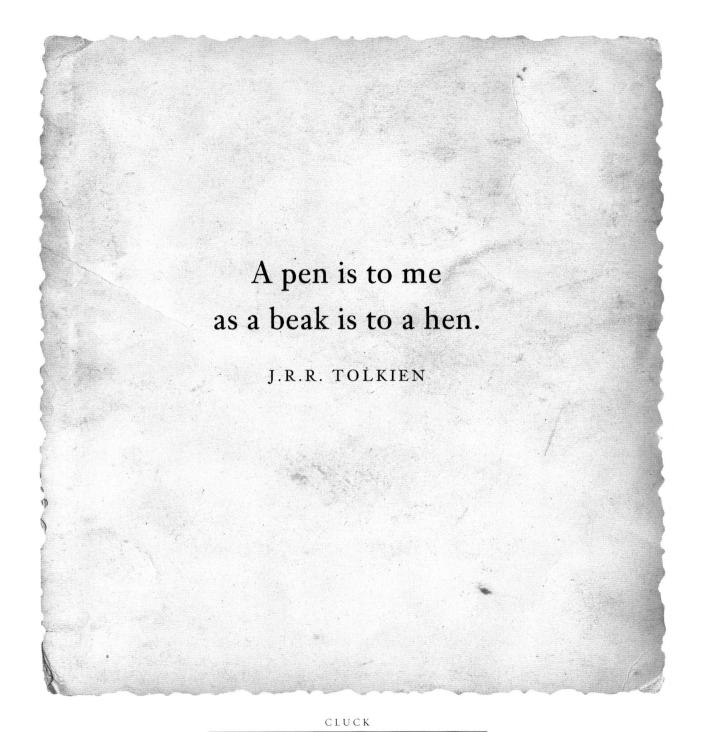

A pen is to me
as a beak is to a hen.

J.R.R. TOLKIEN

Gentleness doesn't get work
done unless you happen to be
a hen laying eggs.

COCO CHANEL

My first business deal was with
my mother. I invested in chickens.
I sold the eggs to my mother.

JOEL MCCREA

Also by Exisle Publishing …

WOOF

A book of happiness for dog lovers

ANOUSKA JONES

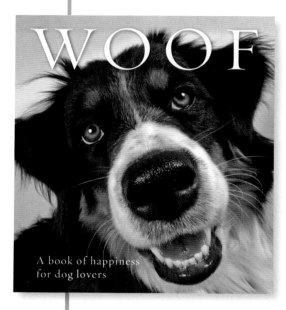

Dogs make our lives feel complete. They're there for us through good times and bad, with their wholehearted engagement in life a lesson to us all on 'living in the moment'.

This is the perfect gift for any dog lover, with its selection of quotes ranging from the serious to the light-hearted, accompanied by beautiful photography.

ISBN 978 1 925335 57 6 (paperback)
ISBN 978 1 925335 09 5 (hardback)

SPIRIT

A book of happiness for horse lovers

ANOUSKA JONES

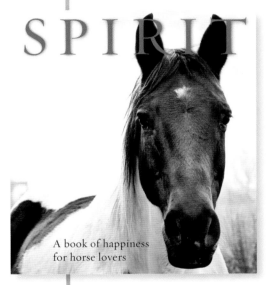

Horses are the epitome of grace, power, and freedom. They also have an ability to touch our souls and connect with our hearts in a way that few other animals can. From a little girl's first pony to a gnarled cowboy's last quarter horse, they can offer us some of our deepest friendships and inspire us to be the best version of ourselves.

Spirit: A book of happiness for horse lovers is a compendium of enduring quotes that capture the essence of our affection for these magnificent animals. Some are by famous people, others not; some are philosophical, others light-hearted — all are memorable. Accompanied by beautiful photography, and presented in a high-quality gift format, this is a collection of quotes to treasure.

ISBN 978 1 921966 95 8 (paperback)
ISBN 978 1 925335 51 4 (hardback)

First published 2018
This edition published 2020

Exisle Publishing Pty Ltd
PO Box 864, Chatswood, NSW 2057, Australia
226 High Street, Dunedin, 9016, New Zealand
www.exislepublishing.com

A CiP record for this book is available from the National Library of Australia.

ISBN 978 1 925820 47 8

Designed by Big Cat Design
Typeset in Archetype 24 on 36pt
Photographs courtesy of Shutterstock
Printed in China

This book uses paper sourced under ISO 14001 guidelines from well-managed forests and other controlled sources.

2 4 6 8 10 9 7 5 3 1

With thanks to the following people for permission to use their quotes: Reuben W. (p. 43); Karen Davis (p. 47); Daniel Pinkwater (p. 55); Lori Hernandez (p. 91); Lara Colley (p. 107); Susan Orlean (p. 119); Nancy Birtwhistle (p. 121); Pippa Greenwood (p. 127); Katherine Center (p. 151).